D1784019

WHAT TO DO ABOUT WORRY

JAY E. ADAMS

PRESBYTERIAN AND REFORMED PUBLISHING CO.
Phillipsburg, New Jersey

ISBN: 0-87552-065-0

WHAT TO DO ABOUT WORRY

Joe used to worry all of the time about everything. His friends all knew him as a worrier. One day Bill was walking down the street when he saw his worrying friend bouncing along as happy as a man could be. Joe was actually whistling and humming and wearing a huge smile; he looked as if he did not have a care in the world. Bill could hardly believe his eyes; it was obvious that a radical transformation had taken place. Bill had known Joe from way back as an inveterate worrier, so he had to find out what had happened.

He stopped Joe and asked, "Joe, what's happened to you? You don't seem worried any more; I never saw a happier man." Joe replied, "It's wonderful Bill, I haven't worried for several weeks now." Bill continued, "That's great; how did you manage it? What brought about the change?" Joe explained, "You see, I hired a man to do all of my worrying for me." "You hired a man to do all of your worrying for you?" "Right," Joe assured him. "Well," Bill mused, "I must say that that is a new wrinkle; tell me, how much does he charge you?" "A thousand dollars a week." "A thousand dollars a week? How could you possibly raise a thousand dollars a week to pay him?" Joe answered, "That's *his* worry."

Wouldn't that be great? Don't you wish it were possible for someone else to handle your worries for you? Well, the Bible says that it is possible; indeed God encourages His children to cast all of their cares on *Him* (I Peter 5:7). And what is best of all—it won't cost you a cent. He freely offers to take your worries and cares upon Himself. Because He does, and because He frequently has ordered us not to worry, all worry is sin. We don't often think about worry as sin. But it is sin because constantly in the Scriptures God tells us not to worry. When we disobey His Word, that is sin. Worry, perhaps, is *the* American sin.

THE EFFECTS OF WORRY

Worry tends to destroy the body. It can put ulcers on the stomach, sap vitality out of living and drive us to an early death. Worry makes us incapable of handling life's problems. Worry keeps us from assuming responsibilities and engaging in activities in the service of Jesus Christ. Worry is sin.

Perhaps you have not overcome worry. Perhaps you are letting worry keep you from serving Jesus Christ as faithfully as you would like. Perhaps you have even reached the point where you worry about your worry! What you want to know is, *what can be done about it?* What does the Bible have to say about overcoming this sin? You want to remove this impediment and—with joy in your heart—learn how to cast your cares on God and serve Him more fully. You can; you really can.

Christian counselors are aware of the fact that many Christians are stymied by this problem. Take Phil, for example. Phil was an engineer who came for counseling. He had been given the task of building a large office building. This assignment was larger than any other he had ever handled, and it was full of problems—problems that he allowed to get to him. He began to worry about them. The worry became so powerful a deterrent to action that one day he simply walked off the job.

The contractors and the subcontractors were fighting; the electricians and the carpenters couldn't get along. Deadlines were not being met. All kinds of difficulties arose. He worried about the job day after day, and as he sat there becoming more and more immobile and less able to handle the day-by-day problems with which he was faced, he himself added to the problems and things went from bad to worse. As he looked at it day after day he finally concluded, "It's just too much; I can't take it." As he saw more and more of the complexities and thought of all of the things that might go wrong, it all finally got to him. Finally one day he laid down his pencil, got up out of his chair, turned around and walked out of the room.

Phil was a Christian. He ended up in our counseling office. As we talked about it, he commented about how destructive worry can be. It could destroy everything that he had worked for. He had been assigned the largest opportunity of his life. He had looked forward to this and worked toward it for years, and he knew that he was capable of doing the job but for one problem—worry. And now it seemed as if worry would destroy all. This is the sort of thing that worry can do.

WHAT WORRY IS

What is worry? In the Bible the word worry usually is translated "anxiety," or "care." It ought to be translated "worry," so that we understand in contemporary language what God is talking about. The Greek word in the New Testament means "to divide, part, rip or tear apart." The word describes the *effects* of worry; that is what worry *does* to us. But worry itself is *concern over the future.* Worry is concern about something that one *can do nothing about,* and that he *cannot even be sure about.* That is why it tears us apart. One who worries looks off into the future. But he finds that as he tries to get hold of it he can't because the future is not here yet. There is no way to grasp it, there is nothing to lay a hand on; there is nothing that can be done. The future is future and the worrier cannot control it; he is not even sure of what it will look like. No one but God knows its true shape. So the worrier worries about what *might* happen. First, he imagines that matters will be this way. But then (he thinks), they might be that way. Because he cannot be sure and cannot control the future, he allows it to tear him apart if he dwells on it and becomes overly concerned about it. That is what worry is according to the Bible: it is concern over the unknown and uncontrollable future that tears one apart. "If that is what worry is," you may say, "what can be done about it?"

WHAT TO DO ABOUT WORRY

Listen to Jesus: He spoke plainly about worry. He has the answer. Jesus directs, "Do not be anxious," i.e., "Do not worry" (Matthew 6:31). But He does not leave the matter there; He goes on to explain how to overcome worry. He concludes a vital discussion concerning anxiety over life's necessities with these tremendously significant words: "Therefore do not be anxious for (worried about) tomorrow, for tomorrow will be anxious for itself" (Matthew 6:34). You see, Jesus made it clear that worry focuses upon tomorrow. That is what is wrong with worry; it is the wrong focus on life. Jesus says that it is wrong to let tomorrow's possible problems tear you apart today.

3

Recognize Tomorrow for What It Is

In this passage Christ contrasts two days. He says first, "Do not worry about tomorrow because tomorrow will take care of itself." Then He emphasizes what has so often been missed, the fact that each day has enough trouble of its own: "Sufficient unto the day is the evil *(trouble,* or *problems)* thereof." In these words you have God's answer to worry. Each day has enough trouble of its own. Don't focus your concern upon tomorrow's problems; there are enough to handle today. The two days indeed are contrasted by Christ. Tomorrow is not for us today; it does not belong to us. Tomorrow always belongs to God. Tomorrow is in His hands, and whenever we try to take hold of it, we try to steal what belongs to Him. Sinners always seem to want, in their perversity, what is not theirs to have.

Today belongs to us. God has not given tomorrow to us today. He has given us only today. He strongly forbids us to become concerned about what *might* happen. That is entirely in His hands. The tragic fact, as we shall see, is that not only do we want what has been forbidden, we also fail to use what has been given to us.

Plan As A Christian

But before we discuss our failure to use today, one point must be made perfectly clear: Christ does not object to the proper kind of planning for tomorrow. He is not opposed to thinking about tomorrow or preparing for tomorrow; what He forbids is worry, the sort of anxiety that tears one to shreds.

There is nothing in Matthew 6 against planning for tomorrow. Nor is there anything against such planning in the book of James. James' words are crucial to an understanding of this matter. James speaks about planning for tomorrow (James 4:13 ff.) and some have mistakenly understood James' words to indicate that he is against all kinds of planning. But that is exactly what he is not against. Indeed, in that passage James is teaching us *how* to plan. He does forbid improper planning, it is true, but at the same time he shows how we may plan as God requires. Planning and worry are two entirely different matters, as Jesus and James both point out.

Listen carefully to what James has to say: "Come now, you who say today or tomorrow we shall go to such and such a city and spend a year there and engage in business there and make a profit." James uses the example of a traveling salesman. He continues: "Yet you do not know what your life will be like tomorrow." "Here you are," he observes, "planning out a whole year's activities, just as if you had control of the future, just as if you knew what the circumstances were going to be, just as if you had a clear picture of that whole year ahead; ridiculous! Worse than that: sinful! You must not do that. Think! You don't even know what tomorrow is going to be like. You may wake up and find out that during the night an earthquake has smashed all of your plans. Everything may change overnight. There are literal earthquakes and personal earthquakes; and they all come so unexpectedly, so suddenly. And not only do you not know what tomorrow will be like, you may not even see tomorrow. You are just a vapor. Like the vapor that appears for a little while and then quickly vanishes away, you are here and gone before you know it. A vapor is the thinnest kind of substance; it is there one moment and then—pfffft!—it's gone. So you have no right to make plans that way."

"How else can one plan?" you might wonder. James supplies the answer to that question. "Instead," he says, "here is how you ought to plan (he doesn't say you ought *not* to plan, but he says instead, there is another way to plan, God's way): you ought to say, *If the Lord wills,* we shall live and also do this or that. But as it is, you boast in your arrogance; all such boasting is evil." Now you see the difference. James says that you must plan (you can't avoid planning), but you must *plan without worry.* Because he acts as if he holds the future in the palm of his hand, the worrier is arrogant. James says that you must plan in such a way that you lay your plans before God and say, "Lord, to the best of my ability I have tried to sketch out my plans according to your will as I have learned it in the Bible, but Lord you are my sovereign God; you are in control of my life; I submit my plans to you. Your will must be done."

As a Christian, you know that you do not really have control of your life. Your life belongs to God by creation. But you also have been bought with a price by the death of Jesus Christ, who gave His life to redeem you from sin and eternal death. In Jesus Christ your very life consists (holds together). Your next breath is in His hands. So you must say, "Lord, this is the plan that I have been able to devise in the light of biblical principles, using the gifts that you have given to me and according to the circumstances as best I can read them. Lord, I lay it before you for your blue penciling." When you plan that way, submitting your plans to the Lord for revision (or scrapping), joyously accepting the scratched-over page that He may hand back to you, then you plan as James says you should; but only then. As our Savior prayed, so must we: "Your will, not mine be done." That is the only way for a Christian to look forward to tomorrow. Planning that is subject to God's alterations fits the words of Christ, because it is planning that does not lead to worry. What is there to worry about when you truly put your best plans into the hands of God?

Focus Your Concern on Today

Now then, let us return to Matthew 6 to discover Jesus' alternative to worry. What can we do about our concern if, as Jesus says, we must not be worried about tomorrow? That is the question: what do we do with our concern? You cannot (must not) turn off concern. This is where so many Christians have given up hope. They know that it is impossible to be free from concern. "How can I turn off my emotions?" they plead. "It is well enough to forbid me to worry, but how do I stop being concerned?" In the answer to that question lies the key to the whole problem of worry. The key that many have missed in talking about worry is this: Christ does not ask you to cease being concerned; instead, He tells you to *redirect your concern*. You must learn how to refocus it. Concern ought not be about tomorrow; such concern tears us apart because we can neither predict nor control tomorrow.

If you have laid your best plans in the Lord's hands, you can turn your attention away from tomorrow. You need no longer be concerned about that, but your concern, your efforts, your energies, all that you have now can be poured into *today*. That is the key that locks the door on worry and opens the door to peace: *focus your concern upon today*.

Concern is right, not wrong. Every emotion that God has put in man is right in its right place. It is right when it is properly used according to the commandments and principles of His Word. While every emotion is right per se, every emotion may be used wrongly. Emotional concern is the God-given ability to mobilize the forces of the body and the mind (for the purpose of), focusing upon and utilizing our energies to solve life's problems. But when we focus upon tomorrow, the chemical and electrical energies of the body are frustrated, because they are poured into the body, but not used. They cannot be released in action, because we cannot *act* upon the future. Rather than releasing bodily energy through productive activity, worry activates more and more energy that is unused, some of which in chemical form may eat away at the lining of the stomach.

All of your time and your energy and your efforts ought to be burned up during today which God has given to you, not transformed into worry about tomorrow which belongs to Him. And if you focus upon today, then you can accomplish something by those efforts. The energy is not wasted, but will be used. Unused acids will not eat away at your stomach, and your concern will count for something. When you focus upon your responsibilities today, your energies can be used fruitfully in the service of Jesus Christ to solve problems rather than to worry about them. That is what Jesus is saying: "Do not be anxious for tomorrow, for tomorrow will care for itself. Each day has enough trouble of its own." Take care of today's problems; take *care* of the troubles that you have to handle now. That is the key to eliminating worry.

Work on Today's Task

Concern for today's problems does not tear you up, *because* you can get a handle on them. You can do something about today's problems. You can do something because they are *here*; you are dealing with concrete reality. Phil, the engineer who walked off his job because of worry, learned that he could do something about today's problems. First, we sat down and looked at the problems, and sketched out a tentative plan for the whole, subject to the Lord's alterations, and put it into His hands in prayer. Then we looked more closely at the coming week to determine (if the Lord wills) what he might do this week. Finally we

7

looked at *today* and asked: "What can be done right now?" Phil was shown that each day God wanted him to look at that day's task and address himself to it. He had been looking at the whole forest and had concluded that it was too dark, too thick, and too large to cut down. Instead, Phil had to learn to say, "By the grace of God those three trees are coming down today." Then, he was to focus and concentrate all of his energy on chopping down those three trees. He must forget the rest. By the end of that day he was to be sure that those three trees were down. The next day he must take down three more, and the following day three more, and possibly the next day four. As he continued to chop them down, three or four a day, the time came when through the forest he began to see daylight on the other side. Phil solved the problem of worry by solving each day's problems one day at a time.

If you work faithfully for Christ, doing what you can about the problems that present themselves today, using all of your energies, and all of your strength and buying up all of the opportunities that He has put at your disposal, you can go home tonight tired but satisfied. How long has it been since you have had that good feeling; not that tired dissatisfied, but that tired-but-satisfied feeling at the end of the day that comes only when you go to bed knowing that you have expended your energies as God has directed you?

There was once a very small fellow who applied for a job as a woodsman out in the Pacific Northwest. He approached the boss (who was a big strapping brute) while he was chatting with a half dozen others of the same sort. The little man said, "I want a job cutting wood." They all began to laugh. "You're too small for this work," the boss replied. But one of the men said, "At least give him a chance to show you what he can do" (it looked like an opportunity to have some fun). The boss, catching on quickly said, "Okay, come over here." He selected one of the largest, hardest trees he could find. He said, "Let's see what you can do with this." Big bruisers gathered all around. They began to whisper, "I couldn't chop that one down in a day!" Another: "Yeah, his axe'll bounce off and hit him in the head." He lifted his axe and, swish— whoofff! Down it came with one clean stroke. The big fellows looked from the tree to the little man in disbelief.

"What's wrong with that tree? Do that again." They took him over to a harder one and a bigger one. Swish—whoofff! Down it came in the same way. "Well," said the boss, "you're hired, but first tell me one thing. Where did you ever learn to cut wood like that?" The little fellow replied, "In the Sahara Forest." "The Sahara Forest? You mean the Sahara Desert, don't you?" The little fellow answered: "That's what they call it *now*." That's just the point, isn't it? One tree here, two trees there, one tree here, three trees there; that is Christ's way. Day by day faithfully working for Jesus Christ will soon change the name of the game. That is the answer to worry according to God's Word.

Do Not Allow Problems to Mount Up

Your shoulders and mine are large enough to carry only one day's problems at a time. This stress upon *one day at a time* is constant throughout the Scriptures. Take a look at one or two passages in which it appears. A good example involves problems that arise between Christian brethren, and this is of particular significance for husbands and wives. To such, the Bible says, "Let not the sun go down on your wrath" (Ephesians 4:26). This means, in effect, settle each day's problems—that day—before you go to bed. Paul is quoting a nighttime Psalm (Psalm 4) in Ephesians 4. Many people seek counseling because they have been building bitterness and resentment for years. You can't carry that sort of load for long without discovering that it destroys you physically and every other way. Test yourself. When you see that the toothpaste tube is squeezed in the middle instead of rolled up from the bottom, what do you say or think? Is your immediate thought "That *woman* (or *man*) has been at it again"? Or do you say, "That *toothpaste tube* is squeezed in the middle"? If it is the former, and particularly if you are emotionally upset over it, then something is wrong. You are bringing more than *that* day's emotion to the problem. It is likely that there are other unsolved problems piled up behind that one.

When Sam sought counseling, he said that he was ready to break up his marriage over such an inconsequential matter. He explained, "My wife always leaves drawers out. Every time I go around a corner, *uhnnh,* I get a stomach full of drawers." That is what he said, and we believed him. But the problem was not only that Sam had a stomach full of drawers; it was bigger than that. He had had a stomach full of his wife!

9

There were many other things involved. If their relationship had been right, Sam and his wife could have solved the drawer issue. It is so simple to solve such problems if both parties are really anxious to *solve* them. You must have the right attitude; you cannot come to the problem with dozens of other unsolved problems backed up behind. That exerts too much pressure. What can you do about toothpaste tubes? Well, if you can't come up with a better solution, at least you could buy his-and-her tubes. You could get a pink one and a blue one, or perhaps green mint Crest and a regular red, white and blue Crest. You can learn to solve many other more complex problems when you do so every day. But the right attitude is basic.

What makes it possible to have the right attitude is keeping accounts current; that is, solving problems each day: "Let not the sun go down on your wrath." Often husbands and wives claim to have sexual problems that basically are not sexual at all. The real problem is that they carry unresolved conflicts into bed at night and yet expect to have good sexual relations. It is difficult for a husband or wife (especially) to make love physically when he (she) doesn't have a good attitude toward the other person. If you haven't solved other problems and you drag all of that baggage into bed with you, it will get in the way. People come for counseling who have let not only the sun, but many moons, go down on their wrath. The Scriptures stress solving problems one day at a time. Just as we cannot bring tomorrow's problems into today, so too we cannot bring yesterday's problems into today: "sufficient unto the day are the problems thereof."

Look at another passage: "Let him deny himself, and take up his cross *daily* and follow me" (Luke 9:23). The Christian life is a daily battle. Daily a Christian must put to death (crucify) his selfish desires and instead follow the will of Christ. Part of that battle is grappling with *today's* problems. Remember, your shoulders are large enough to carry only one day's problems at a time.

THREE STEPS TO DEFEATING WORRY

Now it is important to plug in Philippians 4:4-9. In this passage Paul gives the formula for solving the problem of worry in three plain steps.

Step One – Pray With Thanksgiving

Beginning at Philippians 4:6, note that he says, "Be worried about nothing," *nothing,* that is. There is *never* an excuse for worry. Instead, in *everything* by prayer and supplication with thanksgiving you are to let your requests be made known to God. Every word in the New Testament for prayer is used in that verse. In it Paul speaks of prayer in general, the specific items of concern, earnest entreaty and thanksgiving. In other words, instead of worrying, you must bring both your concern and your concerns about the future to God.

But supplication is not all. If you have missed the startling word in verse six, you have missed the whole point. It is not prayer for solutions to problems (alone) that eliminates worry, rather it is *thankful* prayer for the problem itself. Notice what Paul says: "Be worried about nothing, but in everything by prayer and supplication *with thanksgiving* let your requests be made known." What you are truly thankful for, you do not worry about. Isn't that true? If someone offers to pay a huge hospital bill for you, you stop worrying about the bill. Instead, you are thankful.

"But," you say, "how do I become thankful for *problems?* How do I become thankful for sickness, for loss of salary or employment, for adverse turns of events? I can understand how to be thankful for a gift, but how can I be thankful for trouble?" Well, the answer is found in Romans 8:28: "All things work together for good to those who love God, to those who are the called according to his purpose." The problem is a *gift;* God has said so: "All things work together for *good.*" You must believe this, of course.

If you are a genuine Christian, God has brought you to the place where you have recognized your sin before Him, you have confessed that you have broken His commandments and disobeyed His Word, that you have offended a holy and a righteous God. You have been enabled not only to see your sin, but you also have come for forgiveness to the cross of Jesus Christ. There you have recognized what God did for guilty sinners, and you have personally put your trust in Him. You have repented of your sin and you have cast yourself upon the death of Jesus Christ on the cross for your sins. You know too that God has promised that with Christ He will freely give you *all* things (Romans 8:32). You know that He died to save you from your sins. You know also that Jesus Christ so loved you that He has promised to provide all things necessary to meet your needs (Matthew 6:32). You do not have to carry a load of care any longer. He who died for you did not save you only to abandon you to a hostile world to fend the best way that you can. He says to "seek first his kingdom and his righteousness, and all these things shall be added to you" (Matthew 6:33). The King of all, who began a good work in you will perfect it until the day of His revelation as King. He works in your life continually. According to His promise He cares for you. Your King has so ordered "all things" for those He has saved that *all* things (those problems, those troubles, those heartaches, those sorrows, that grief), *all* things work together for good. You must believe that. Your sovereign God controls all things and orders them all so that they work together for your good. Then even when you don't see how, you can't understand why, and you are unable to grasp the whole picture, you must believe Him. When the pain is so great that you can't *imagine* how it works for good, you can still *believe* Him. That is what faith is all about (cf. Matthew 6:25-30; especially verse 30). And you can give thanks.

One day John was invited by Fred to visit his tapestry shop where, he was told, beautiful tapestries were on display. As John entered the large display room he was struck by a huge tapestry stretched from the four corners of a balcony up above. His guide remarked, "This is the loveliest tapestry of all." John looked up at it and couldn't believe what he saw; it was a hideous tangled mess of thread. He thought, "That is without a doubt the ugliest tapestry that I ever saw; it is a meaningless web of discolor and disharmony." He said, "Fred, I can't understand why you would hang up an ugly thing like that." Fred replied, "Wait a minute John; withhold your judgment." He then led him up the stairs to the balcony. "Now," he asked as they looked over the rail, "What do you think?" Below was the upper side of the tapestry on which was woven the most magnificent pattern John had ever seen. Yet it had been woven with those same threads that from below seemed so disordered. Now he could *see* the gorgeous pattern of breathtaking beauty.

You now look at the underneath side of life. Often you can't understand God's plan; it looks tangled, garbled, ugly. But some day you shall know as you are known; you will see things as God sees them. You will understand the purpose of each dark thread. You will see that it was truly a beautiful and necessary part of the whole pattern. It, indeed, was working together for your *good.* Sometimes here God allows a glimpse of the pattern, but then you will see the whole in all of its perfection. When you know this you can thank God for problems; you can pray with thanksgiving instead of worrying.

Step Two – Find God's Solutions to Problems

The second thing that God says in Philippians 4 is to set your mind on positive biblical solutions to life's problems. Notice Philippians 4:8: "Finally, brethren, whatever is true, whatever is honorable, whatever is pure, whatever is lovely, whatever is of good report, if there is any excellence, if there is anything worthy of praise, let your mind dwell on these things." This is not Norman Vincent Pealeism; this is Paul writing to the Philippians. This is the Word of God putting the finger on the main problem in the life of many worried Christians.

We have already seen one way in which worriers focus their minds on the wrong things; they center upon tomorrow rather than on today. Here is another. Often people who seek counseling are depressed and immobilized. They may have stopped working for God, and they may have given up on life. Frequently they get that way because when problems pile up they begin to worry about these in self pity. Sometimes they wallow deep in it with both feet. Self pity and worry are kissing cousins. Worriers tend to focus on problems rather than on solutions. They spend much time exploring new avenues of each problem themselves. Some also talk to their friends about their troubles, and as they rehash them they have an opportunity to shake their heads all over again. Paul says that if you want to have peace, if you want to get rid of worry, you must not spend your time thinking or talking about the dark, the dull and the miserable side of life. That does not mean that you are to become a Christian Scientist who denies the existence of evil. But what it does mean is that after having taken a hard realistic look at each problem, rather than indulging in self pity, you must then search for God's solution to it. You must find the positive things that you can do; the things that are good and true and right and pure. Every problem has its upper side. Ask questions like, "What good can be brought out of this?" "How can I handle it to bring honor to God?"

Much advice given to counselors concerning ventilation and talking about problems is quite erroneous. Talk can be one of the most destructive forces in life. The worst you could do if you counsel another is to *talk* to him about his problems. Take this tip to heart: don't ever talk to anybody about his problems. Does that advice puzzle you? Were you led to think that talk is "therapeutic"? Let's consider that idea for a moment. Take an example. Here is a man who has a problem, and he has been worrying about it. He has been wallowing in self pity. You talk to him about his problem. What are you doing? Probably you are giving him some new insights into the depths of his problem, you are probably showing him new angles that had not occurred to him before, etc. He may get a temporary ten-minute (or even ten-hour) relief from getting it off his chest. But when he begins to reflect on the problem again, he now sees how much larger it has become. You have helped to *increase* his problem. It was big before; now it is huge. Talking about problems—*merely* talking about problems—is like tearing off a scab and poking a finger down into the bloody mess; it only aggravates the difficulty. Such talk is destructive because it centers on the problem.

You say, "But I thought counselors were supposed to talk about problems." Very well, they are; but not merely to talk about *problems.* They must learn always to talk *through* problems to biblical *solutions.* You must learn to do the same to conquer worry. You must focus upon what God says should be *done* about problems. You must not focus just upon the problem or how bad it is. A biblical counselor sympathizes, but he knows that real sympathy means helping another to dig through to God's answer. The task of excavating the treasures of the Scriptures to help another to find the answer is harder than commiserating over the problem. But that is what is involved in helping somebody who has problems. If a counselor is unable or unwilling to do this, he should not be a counselor. You see, then, that to stop worrying you need to focus on the positive side, on solutions rather than upon the gravity of the problem.

14

Thirdly, Paul insists, "The things that you have learned and received and heard and seen in me, practice, and the God of peace shall be with you" (Philippians 4:9). Here is the final step to peace. First comes prayer with thanksgiving, then a focus upon what can be done about problems. Now Paul says that you must go to work on the problem; you must do the things that God says must be done to solve it. The solution involves work; don't miss that. The final solution to *worry* is *work*. No man who really grapples with problems is a worrying man. God has made our bodies with a two-sided nervous system. You automatically switch one on as you switch the other off. One is the worrying side and the other is the working side. And if you are really working on today's problem, you cannot worry about what might (but probably won't) happen tomorrow. You must pour your energies, your efforts, and your whole person into solving today's problems. Put all of your concern *there*.

You probably won't believe this until you see it for yourself, but do you know that the Scriptures indicate that many worrying people are *lazy?* Well, that is what Jesus Himself said concerning one worrier who was afraid of the future, and sought to be excused from his present responsibilities on the basis of such fear. Instead, Jesus called him lazy. In Matthew 25, Christ told the story of three servants who were given money to invest. When their Lord returned, he inquired about their investments. The one who had been given the most doubled the amount, and the second did the same. But the third confessed that he hid his money in the ground. When the Lord returned he dug it up, brought it to him and said, "Here is your money, Lord. I buried it because I was afraid" (vs. 25). The slave worried about the possible consequences of investing the money. He worried about what might happen if he should lose rather than gain. He worried about what the Lord might say or do. He worried and worried, and worried, and became paralyzed. He worried and did not work. But his master answered, "You wicked (note, it is sinful to worry), lazy slave . . . You ought to have put my money in the bank, and on my arrival I would have received my money back with interest" (Matthew 25:25, 26), i.e., "At least you should have done the minimal thing you could, but you didn't. You are a lazy slave."

You see, the worrier doesn't have to *do* anything; indeed he *can't* do anything because he is working on tomorrow's problem. But that really boils down to no work at all. You can't do anything about problems that are yet in the future. Worrying is like rocking in a rocking chair; you expend a lot of energy but you don't get anywhere. You say, "Oh my, this is a serious problem! It is really terrible. I've already spent eight hours worrying about it. Oh my; oh my." Worriers then are often (perhaps always) lazy people. *Something* can always be *done* about a problem (cf. I Corinthians 10:13). Even if you can't change a thing outside of yourself, by the sanctifying power of the Holy Spirit your attitudes toward problems and your behavioral responses toward them can be changed. *You* can change in the situation if nothing else will. There is always something, then, that can be done.

Here is a simple procedure that you might want to use when you find yourself worrying instead of working. Instead of worrying, immediately sit down and write out the following three questions on a piece of paper, leaving spaces beneath each so that you can fill them in later. You might even have a few of these sheets mimeographed for yourself and put them on your desk or carry them in your pocket. We have made it possible for you to begin right away by printing ten sheets in this booklet.* The questions are:

1. What is my problem?

2. What does God want me to do about it?

3. When, where and how should I begin?

---

*You will notice that ten sheets have been provided for your use at the end of this booklet. Counselors may wish to have counselees fill these in and bring them to subsequent counseling sessions.

Sometimes just defining a problem by forcing yourself to write it out leads to a solution. When it is defined you must begin immediately to look for the solution in the Scriptures. Look for the positive side. Ask, "How can I handle this problem for the glory of God?" But then, don't settle for good solutions and noble ideals; get to work. Schedule your actions and put the hardest task first. Don't forget Abraham, who got up *early*, the Scriptures say, when he was given the heartrending command to sacrifice Isaac, his only son, whom he loved (Genesis 22:3). There you have God's solution to worry.

ONE REASON FOR WORRY

One final thought: this booklet is written for Christians, but if it should happen that you do not know Jesus Christ as your Savior, let me say one word to you. While God says that Christians do not have anything to worry about, you have *everything* to worry about. There is no such promise as that in Romans 8:28 for you. That promise was made exclusively to God's own: "all things work together for good *to those who love God.*" There is no solution to your problems apart from Jesus Christ. There is nothing but unending hell at the end of your road. "Well," you say, "then I'll have plenty of company." That is the way that many joke about hell, I know. But have you really read what the Bible says about that question? Not only does it describe hell as a lake of fire and brimstone, a place where the worm dies not and a place where people will weep and wail and gnash their teeth in pain, but it also pictures hell (in what are perhaps the most fearful terms of all) as a place of utter darkness and loneliness. Persons in hell are like wandering stars, light years away from each other! (Jude 13). Think of the loneliness! And worse still, you will wander forever in isolation and darkness from the presence of God: "And these will pay the penalty of eternal destruction, away from the presence of the Lord and from the glory of His power" (II Thessalonians 1:9). That is the most terrible fact of all. Hell is going to be an extremely lonely place where men, instead of worrying about the future, will anguish in memory of the past. There alone is the future certain; there the terror of an everlasting future apart from God will be the awful certainty.

17

But perhaps God has been working in your heart to convict you of your sin. Possibly He has put this pamphlet into your hands because He wants you to put your trust in Jesus Christ. Why don't you do so right now? Don't merely worry—act! Act in obedience to the Word of God.

To those of you who know Him, let me ask, "Do you need to repent of the sin of worry?" Do so, then take each day's problems as they come, and do business that day for Jesus Christ.

1. What is my problem?

2. What does God want me to do about it?

3. When, where and how should I begin?

1. What is my problem?

2. What does God want me to do about it?

3. When, where and how should I begin?

1. What is my problem?

2. What does God want me to do about it?

3. When, where and how should I begin?

1. What is my problem?

2. What does God want me to do about it?

3. When, where and how should I begin?

1. What is my problem?

2. What does God want me to do about it?

3. When, where and how should I begin?

1. What is my problem?

2. What does God want me to do about it?

3. When, where and how should I begin?

1. What is my problem?

2. What does God want me to do about it?

3. When, where and how should I begin?

1. What is my problem?

2. What does God want me to do about it?

3. When, where and how should I begin?

1. What is my problem?

2. What does God want me to do about it?

3. When, where and how should I begin?

1. What is my problem?

2. What does God want me to do about it?

3. When, where and how should I begin?